Hung Your Tongue

WORDS HAVE POWER
WHAT DID YOU SAY?

Patricia Pope-Jackson

TRILOGY CHRISTIAN PUBLISHERS
TUSTIN, CA

TRILOGY

Trilogy Christian Publishers
A Wholly Owned Subsidary of Trinity Broadcasting Network
2442 Michelle Drive
Tustin, CA 92780

Library of Congress Cataloging-in-Publication Data is available.

ISBN 978-1-63769-342-1

ISBN 978-1-63769-343-8 (ebook)

Contents

Acknowledgements

I am giving honor to God and thanking him for being the Lord of my life. On my sophomore effort, I am thanking Him for giving me this title and helping me to bring forth this project with His Word.

To my parents, Bennie and Bernice—I love you dearly. I am so glad God gave me you as parents. I've had nothing but a blessed life! Thank you, mother, for raising us up in church! To my siblings, Cynthia and Butch, I love you! To my husband, Jolus, and son, Marquise, I love you and thank God for you!

To the TBN Staff—thank you for helping me bring forth another project! God bless you all!

To my pastors, Dr. Creflo and Taffi Dollar, what can I say? You are the best, and I am glad God assigned me to your church! I love you to life!

WORDS

Words are the most powerful force available to humanity. We can choose to use them constructively with words of encouragement or destructively use words of despair. Words have the power to help, to heal, to hinder, to hurt, to harm, to humiliate, or to humble. Words kill, words give life, they're either poison or fruit—you choose!

Words are more powerful than actions. With words, you can influence someone into thinking something. It is the way we communicate and learn. Words can allow someone to take over your mind completely, while actions can only force you to do something out of fear.

"Whoever of you loves life and desires to see many good days, keep your tongue from evil and your lips from telling lies" (Psalm 34:12-13, NIV).

"The mouth of the righteous is a fountain of life *and* his words of wisdom are a source of blessing, But the mouth of the wicked conceals violence *and* evil" (Proverbs 10:11, AMP).

Words, we speak them every day, whether talking with friends and family or in business. We use them to bind a business contract we sign or when shaking hands when we agree upon a business endeavor. God made us speaking spirits, so we must be careful about what we say! Words have so much power, so do not let negative ones come out of your mouth. In the first book of the Bible, Genesis stated how God "said, and He saw," and since He made us in His image, we can do the same thing, say, and we see!

"You are snared by the words of your mouth; You are taken by the words of your mouth." (Proverbs 6:2, NKJV)

"Kind words heal and help; cutting words wound and maim" (Proverbs 15:4, MSG).

"Gracious words are like a honeycomb, sweetness to the soul and health to the body" (Proverbs 16:24, ESV).

"The words of a man's mouth are as deep waters, and the wellspring of wisdom as a flowing brook" (Proverbs 18:4, KJV).

We must be careful of the words we speak because what we say, we will have. If we look at our life, our life is the sum total of the words we have spoken. We are all a work in progress. None of us are totally there yet, but keep moving forward. We can either bless people with our words or curse them when we speak ill of them.

"But the tongue can no man tame; it is an unruly evil, full of deadly poison" (James 3:8, KJV).

This is scary: You can tame a tiger, but you can't tame a tongue—it's never been done. The tongue runs wild, a wanton killer. With our tongues we bless God our Father; with the same tongues we curse the very men and women he made in his image. Curses and blessings out of the same mouth!

My friends, this can't go on. A spring doesn't gush fresh water one day and brackish the next, does it? Apple trees don't bear strawberries, do they? Raspberry bushes don't bear apples, do they? You're not going to dip into a polluted mud hole and get a cup of clear, cool water, are you?

James 3:7-12 (MSG)

The Mouth

Our mouth is very powerful. We must always think before we speak. Thoughts proceed actions, then a lot of the time we will speak what we were thinking. Right thinking equals right believing, which equals right speaking!

Our thoughts and words come from what we believe, so we are being pulled toward what we think and speak over ourselves. Are you speaking words of life, faith, and victory, or are you thinking and speaking defeat, loss, and mediocrity?

"Set a guard over my mouth, *LORD*; keep watch over the door of my lips" (Psalm 141:3, NIV).

"The one who guards his mouth [thinking before he speaks] protects his life;

The one who opens his lips wide [and chatters without thinking] comes to ruin" (Proverbs 13:3, AMP).

Lord, put a guard over our mouths! There is power in your mouth. You will have what you say, so what are you saying?

There was a saying when I was growing up that I would say as a child, you are more than likely familiar with it. It goes:

Sticks and stones may break my bones
But words will never harm me!

Not true! Words can *kill you!*

What to Speak

When you are sick in your body, is Jesus your first choice? Jesus died for every sickness known to man, and by His stripes, you were healed! Which means we are already healed! Since you are already healed, pray from the standpoint that I am the healed protecting my health. Jesus, you took all my infirmities, so I am already healed as it manifests in Jesus' name. I've had supernatural healing as well as God working through the doctors for my manifestation. You cannot tell God how to heal you, just know that you already are and receive it in Jesus' name!

I've heard a prophet say, "God keeps telling my people: you could have what you say (His promises), but you keep saying what you have (the problem)!"

What do you speak over yourself? Do you speak the circumstance? Or do you speak the promise over the problem!

Don't look at the circumstance (the circle you are standing in)

Look at what the Word says over your circumstance!

For the Bible says:

"Herein is our love made perfect, that we may have boldness in the day of judgment: because as He is, so are we in this world" (1 John 4:17, KJV). "This is how love is made complete among us so that we will have confidence on the day of judgment: In this world, we are like Jesus" (1 John 4:17, NIV).

Look at Jesus when you are going through, so if it isn't on Jesus, then it isn't on *you!*

If you ever get an evil report from the doctor, don't receive it! You let the doctor know. Oh *no*, My God says I am healed! I know a doctor that has never lost a patient! *His* name is *Jesus.* Open your mouth and say what God says about you, "I'm *healed* in Jesus' *name!*" I've told several doctors that no matter how strange they may look at me, I am not ashamed of who I am and whose I am!

So, what to speak? Speak God's Word over every facet of your life! It has so much power! It is a living *word!*

Patricia's Testimony—Confessing the Word—the Healing Power

I have a personal testimony about this! I was given such a report that I would not receive even though it showed up! The diabetes testimony. Sickness is an evil report!

It was November 2019, I went to the doctor, and my test results had numbers going all kinds of ways.

When I took the A1C test, my doctor said, "Mrs. Jackson, you have diabetes." I told her, "No...I don't!" She said, "Oh yes, the A1C percentage was 7 percent." I told her respectfully, "That is what you say...My God says I am healed!"

She said, "I want to see you back in March 2020." I said, "Okay, but I do not have diabetes." Now, did it show up? Yes! Would I receive it? No! I went on a regiment because I was eating all kinds of stuff I shouldn't have, but I also said, "I'm just like Jesus...He has no sickness, and neither do I!"

In March 2020, I came back to check my A1C, and it went down to 6.6 percent. She said, "I don't know what you're doing but keep it up!" I told her it was Jesus!

She said, "I want you to come back in June 2020." I said, "Okay," and then I said, "by the way, what is the percentage that states your blood sugar is normal?" She stated, "6.5 percent and under." I said, "Okay, when I see you in June, I will be under 6.5 percent."

I came back in June 2020, took the A1C...my result from the A1C was 6.4 percent. I said, "I told you I don't have diabetes." She was astounded! I told her this is God! Jesus! I give him all the praise! As you see, I would not receive it because I did not have it! I only had what I said. Stay consistent on God's promises!

When the doctor says to you about your diabetes or your sickness, you tell them respectfully, "No, I don't own any sickness! What I own is my house, my car, and besides those items, I own healing!" Don't ever say "my" when it comes to sickness because you don't own it!

I heard a testimony about a lady that was diagnosed with an aggressive form of cancer, and she was scheduled to have surgery. She went home and got a hold of the Scripture, "As he is, so am I in this world," and she said, "Wait a minute, I'm just like God! If He isn't sick, then neither am I!" When she went to have the surgery, the doctors were astounded. They could not find any trace of cancer! I was rejoicing for her! God, I give You praise! I must say this again...Do you see how powerful your mouth is with the *Word* in it?

Keep in mind that a "symptom" is not a sickness until you turn it into one with your mouth! Can you see how powerful words and your mouth are? If someone says, "Oh, are you catching a cold?" Your response should be, "No, the only thing I am catching is healing! I'm not catching any sickness!" And like I said, this is a practice, but you will get there!

Always *cancel* a negative report! You say:

I Cancel That

If the doctor says you have a disease, You say, "In the name of Jesus, I *cancel* that! I am healed in Jesus' name!"
If your finances say you are in lack,
You say, "In the name of Jesus, I *cancel* that; I am rich in Jesus' name! I am blessed to be a blessing!"

You Will Have What You Say, *Not* What You Mean!

Testimony 2—About My Aunt and Uncle—1989

I want to tell you a story about some close family members. I grew up in church but was not saved at the time and was not into the Word when this happened. This was my first encounter with how powerful words were. This happened back in 1989. My parents moved to New York in the 1950s, had the three of us, worked, and then, upon their retirement, was planning to move back home to South Carolina. So many times, they would tell my Aunt and Uncle (my mom's brother) that yes, we are coming back home to live. It was now 1989, and they told them at the end of this year, they would be moving back. My uncle said out of his mouth, "Bernice and Bennie...chile about time you move back here we would probably be dead!" Well, moving on to Thanksgiving of 1989, my uncle took his wife to the hospital that Saturday after Thanksgiving because she was not feeling well. In the midst of him checking her in and then heading back home, he dropped dead of a massive heart attack in the hospital. My aunt did not know it at the time, by the time she found out that following Monday, he had passed away, she passed away later on that day. And would you know that my parents moved back to South Carolina the week of their death! They moved back to South Carolina then. I will never forget this; that is when I first thought about words and their power. My uncle did not realize that those words would manifest, and they both would be gone by the time my parents moved back! My parents came back to a double funeral of my mom's brother and her sister-in-law.

"Death and life *are* in the power of the tongue: and they that love it shall eat the fruit thereof" (Proverbs 18:21, KJV).

What Are You Saying?

If you are defeated in your thoughts, you will be defeated in your life! You will speak the wrong words out of your mouth! The wrong words are so easy to say, so you have to be cognizant of what you say. You have to be so mindful, especially when you are in a setting with your family or friends. We are more likely then to say the wrong thing and things we don't mean. I had to be very careful in those settings because you can say things and wonder...where did that come from?

Some of the wrong things people say:

"My feet are killing me"—Really? *No!* Your feet are hurting you, but you are healed in Jesus' name!

"You make me sick"—No, you don't! You may irritate me, but you will not make me sick!

"I thought I would die laughing"—No, I won't!

"I'm so stupid"—No, you're not! However, if you keep on saying that, you will become progressively stupid!

"You are so crazy"—*No!* You are so funny!

You will never be anything—(some people say this to their children out of anger) dear God, do not say that! You should say—The possibilities are endless for you in your life, the sky is not the limit!

Speak a blessing over yourself! That is what *"you say"!*

"So (it shall be) that he who invokes a blessing on himself in the land shall do so by saying" (Isaiah 65:16, AMPC).

"That he who blesseth himself in the earth shall bless himself in the God of truth" (Isaiah 65:16, KJV).

Testimony 3—COVID-19—January 2021

My dad, who is ninety-three and is an Army Veteran, qualifies for assistance because of his veteran status. We have had several home attendants come to the house to take care of him. The last one we had to assist was exposed to COVID (later on, he did contract COVID). He would come on Monday, Wednesday, and Friday. He was last here on a Monday. The following Tuesday, I got a call for the family to get tested. When I tell you I was as calm as a cucumber, I couldn't get any calmer than that! I was so happy and ready to go! That may sound odd, but I was! Let me tell you why. At the start of the pandemic shutdown, my pastors were making confessions weekly (Monday, Tuesday, Thursday, Friday) and are still doing them. They started in March 2020. I did start in March 2020 but did not start consistently until April 2020. We would confess Psalm 91 "every" day. We made other confessions, but Psalm 91 was confessed every day over me and "my" house. We are Psalm 91 equipped! To this day, we are still confessing Psalm 91! You see, because of these *"words"* (the Word of God) and our "confessing" (speaking), this house is protected, and *nothing* by *any* means shall hurt us! The Word made me so calm!

I said, "family, we do not have COVID, and we never will because I know the Word is sharper than a two-edged sword, and it will accomplish what it is set out to do! I was so happy to take a COVID test because *I know* that, *I know* that, *I know* we were negative! We all had exactly what we were confessing (my mom confessed with me too); I and my house were *negative! Thank you, Jesus!* See, when you get in the *Word* and get it in your heart, no *one* can tell you anything! The Word and speaking works!

Get Psalm 91 equipped:

He that dwelleth in the secret place of the most High shall abide under the shadow of the Almighty.

I will say of the LORD, He is my refuge and my fortress: my God; in him will I trust.

Surely he shall deliver thee from the snare of the fowler, and from the noisome pestilence.

He shall cover thee with his feathers, and under his wings shalt thou trust: his truth shall be thy shield and buckler.

Thou shalt not be afraid for the terror by night; nor for the arrow that flieth by day;

Nor for the pestilence that walketh in darkness; nor for the destruction that wasteth at noonday.

A thousand shall fall at thy side, and ten thousand at thy right hand; but it shall not come nigh thee.

Only with thine eyes shalt thou behold and see the reward of the wicked.

Because thou hast made the LORD, which is my refuge, even the most High, thy habitation;

There shall no evil befall thee, neither shall any plague come nigh thy dwelling.

For he shall give his angels charge over thee, to keep thee in all thy ways.

They shall bear thee up in their hands, lest thou dash thy foot against a stone.

Thou shalt tread upon the lion and adder: the young lion and the dragon shalt thou trample under feet.

Because he hath set his love upon me, therefore will I deliver him: I will set him on high, because he hath known my name.

He shall call upon me, and I will answer him: I will be with him in trouble; I will deliver him, and honour him.

With long life will I satisfy him and shew him my salvation.

Psalm 91 (KJV)

Are you decreeing anything over your life? For your family?

"Thou shalt also decree a thing, and it shall be established unto thee: and the light shall shine upon thy ways" (Job 22:28, KJV).

What are you decreeing? What are you establishing? Healing for those who have been afflicted? Salvation for your unsaved loved ones?

Father, I thank you in the name of Jesus that all my unsaved family members and friends are saved, sanctified, and filled with the Holy Spirit! Father, they just love the church and the Word!

The Law of Confession—You will have what you say, so speak over your loved one's life! Say what God says! Speak His Word!

For when the enemy tries to come against you through your mind, remember what Jesus did for us:

"And Jesus, having disarmed the powers and authorities of Satan, he made a public spectacle of him, triumphing over him by the cross" (Colossians 2:15, NIV)

Don't let someone who is defeated defeat you! Don't give him *your power!*

You open your mouth with the Word:

I have the mind of Christ!

Greater is he that is in you than he that is in the world!

God always causes me to triumph in Christ Jesus!

When Satan tries to give you a crazy thought, seal your mind by saying:

In the name of Jesus, I take the blood, and I seal the door of my mind from that thought ever coming back again!

It's *warfare, but we win!* It's three against one — Father, Spirit, Son!

Enough said!

For verily I say unto you, that whosoever shall say unto this mountain, Be thou removed, and be thou cast into the sea; and shall not doubt in his heart, but shall believe that those things which he saith shall come to pass; he shall have whatsoever he saith.

Mark 11:23 (KJV)

God wants to blow our minds with His goodness, so we need to think and speak big! The sky is not the limit!

I speak the impossible, meaning it is impossible for me to do *but God!* He can do *anything!*

When I lived in Georgia, I would go to Walmart and say thank you, Lord; I can buy *everything* in this store! Father, I thank you. I can buy every Walmart in the state of Georgia! I did the same thing when I moved to South Carolina!

When I was in my house in Georgia, I would say, "Lord, I thank you, I can pay off everybody's mortgage in my subdivision! And I still have plenty more in store. I am blessed to be a *blessing!*"

Take the Limits off God! He wants to bless you! You can't be a blessing if you're not blessed! How can you help someone if you need help?

How God Sees You?

We should always look at ourselves on how God sees us. He sees us as righteous! Not because of what we did, it is because of what Jesus did! He sees us through the eyes of *Jesus!* Jesus, I so thank you for what you have done for me! I am the righteousness of God because of what you did. You cannot undo your righteousness because you did not make yourself righteous! Jesus made you righteous when you accepted Him! I so love you, *Jesus!* This is about receiving, believing, how God sees you!

How Do You See Yourself?

Is it how God sees you? Is it what He says about you? Honor Him for what He says about you!

You're the righteousness of God.

The apple of His eye.

Healed.

Fearfully and wonderfully made.

In peace—He would keep us in perfect peace as our mind stays on Him.

No fear—He gives us power, love, and a sound mind.

God loads us daily with benefits. He is our salvation.

I am successful and prosperous. I meditate on God's Word day and night.

God makes all grace abound toward me so that I always have all sufficiency and an abundance for every good work.

God abundantly blesses my provision.

The Lord causes my enemies who rise against me to be defeated before my face; they come out against me one way and flee before me seven ways.

The Lord commands His blessing on my storehouses, and in all that I set my hand to do, and He blesses me in the land that He is giving me.

All of this is in His Word! Read it, live it! Let it wash you and change your life!

What is Your Vision?

Have you written it down? Have you made it plain? A man without a vision will perish! I have written my vision down, and as it manifest, I check it off! I decree it, and then I speak the vision out of my mouth! I know I will have what I say, so I speak it, but most of all, I believe it! Write it, read it, speak it! God is so awesome! He has put in His *Word* everything that pertains to life as well as His instructions to live this life! If you would pick up your Bible or, with today's technology, your cell phone, iPad, or tablet, you will or can transform your life. Use the world's technology to bless you!

"And the LORD answered me, and said, Write the vision, and make it plain upon tables" (Habakkuk 2:2, KJV).

"Where there is no vision, the people perish" (Proverbs 29:18, KJV).

"According as His divine power hath given unto us all things that pertain unto life and godliness, through the knowledge of Him that hath called us to glory and virtue" (2 Peter 1:3, KJV).

God Has Given Us All Things That Pertain to Life and Godliness:
- God's Word, the Bible.
- Forgiveness of sins through the death of Christ.
- The right to pray.
- The necessities of life.
- Parents to guide us in our youth.
- The angels to minister to us.

Angels React to Your Words

"Bless the Lord, you His angels, who excel in strength, who do His Word, heeding the voice of His Word" (Psalm 103:20, NKJV).

"Bless the LORD, you His angels, You mighty ones who do His commandments, Obeying the voice of His Word!" (Psalm 103:20, AMP)

Are you giving voice to His *Word*? Are you giving your angels anything to carry out or do? Some of these angels have a load of dust on them because you have not said anything. Thank you, Lord, for making it so simple to speak your Word in order to bring it to life! What an awesome God we serve!

How is Your Love Walk?

Are you walking in love? Treating people right? Saying words of affirmation and speaking the blessings over their life? God is concerned over every aspect of our life. He is into the little things, every detail, and most certainly cares how we treat and speak about people as well as how we speak to them. Don't grieve the Holy Spirit in your love walk! Ask yourself, how would you feel if you were treated or spoke to in that matter? If you wouldn't like it, then neither would they! Speak life and blessings!

Communion

I decided to add this to the book because it is so important. Have you taken communion over issues that arise in your life? It is so powerful to do. It is not just for Sunday. It can be for any day. I have taken it for family, friends, specific situations. I've spoken words over them and have seen the change! Sometimes, God would say to me, take it for seven days over certain issues, or I would wake up in the morning, and He would say take communion today. It is so powerful. Take communion and watch how your situation and problems change! There is healing power in communion! *All is well* with everything that concerns you!

Keep Your Confessions in the Present Tense!

Faith is *now*!

Keep your confessions in the faith tense, which is "now," by saying "*I am*"!

This is what *I am right now*:

I am a victor.

"No, in all these things, we are more than conquerors through Him who loved us."

I am designed for good works.

"For we are God's handiwork, created in Christ Jesus to do good works, which God prepared in advance for us to do."

I am a co-heir with Christ.

"Now if we are children, then we are heirs—heirs of God and co-heirs with Christ. If indeed we share in

His sufferings in order that we may also share with His glory."

I am the salt of the earth.

"You are the salt of the earth."

I am a new creation.

"Therefore, if anyone is in Christ, he is a new creation. The old has gone, the new has come."

I am reconciled in Christ! My message is reconciliation and freedom.

"All this is from God, who reconciled us to Himself through Christ and gave us the ministry of reconciliation: that God was reconciling the world to Himself in Christ, not counting people's sins against them. And He has committed to us the message of reconciliation."

I am righteous and holy.

"And to put on the new self, created to be like God in true righteousness and holiness."

I am saved by grace as a gift, not because of my performance.

"God saved you by His grace when you believed. And you can't take credit for this; it is a gift from God.

I am chosen and called by God to produce fruit.

"You did not choose me, but I chose you and appointed you so that you might go and bear fruit—fruit that will last—and so that whatever you ask in my name the Father will give you.

I have royalty in my veins and lead with integrity.

"But you are a chosen people, a royal priesthood, a holy nation, God's special possession, that you may declare the praises of Him who called you out of darkness into His wonderful light."

I have a heavenly calling.

"Therefore, holy brothers and sisters, who share in the heavenly calling, fix your thoughts on Jesus, whom we acknowledge as our apostle and high priest."

I am a vessel of Divine Light.

"For God, who said, "Let light shine out of darkness," made His light shine in our hearts to give us the light of the knowledge of God's glory displayed in the face of Christ."

I am accepted in the beloved. Having predestinated us unto the adoption of children by Jesus Christ to Himself, according to the good pleasure of His will, To the praise of the glory of His grace, wherein He hath made us accepted in the beloved.

Your Life

Everything in life deals with words, speaking them, confessing them. You have the control over your life by what you say! Keep the right words in your mouth, and you will have an awesome life! Only you can make this happen by speaking right! If you don't know what to say, then say nothing. I rather have a closed mouth than a mouth that speaks wrong, and I give life to those words. It was stated that some people have a mouth and don't know what to do with it! Let that not be you! Speak the *Word only*!

Outro

In closing, I want to leave you with this:

Hung by your tongue, there is power in your mouth! Change your words—change your life!

Scriptures to Know

"Put away from you crooked speech and put devious talk far from you" (Proverbs 4:24, ESV).

"The mouth of the righteous is a fountain of life, but the mouth of the wicked conceals violence" (Proverbs 10:11, ESV).

"The words of the wicked lie in wait for blood, but the mouth of the upright delivers them" (Proverbs 12:6, ESV).

"The lips of the righteous feed many, but fools die for lack of sense" (Proverbs 10:21, ESV).

Let God be true, and every human being a liar. As it is written:
"So that you may be proved right when you speak

and prevail when you judge.
Romans 3:4 (NIV)

"For 'Whoever desires to love life and see good days, let him keep his tongue from evil and his lips from speaking deceit'" (1 Peter 3:10, ESV).

"But whatever [Word] comes out of the mouth comes from the heart, and this is what defiles and dishonors the man" (Matthew 15:18, AMP).

By this you know the Spirit of God: every spirit that confesses that Jesus Christ has come in the flesh is from God, and every spirit that does not confess Jesus is not from God. This is the spirit of the antichrist, which you heard was coming and now is in the world already.
1 John 4:2-3 (ESV)

"Let your speech always be gracious, seasoned with salt, so that you may know how you ought to answer each person" (Colossians 4:6, ESV).

When the Spirit of truth comes, he will guide you into all the truth, for he will not speak on his own authority, but whatever he hears he will speak, and he will declare to you the things that are to come.
John 16:13 (ESV)